Let's Read About...
Pocahontas

For Keith, with love
—K.W.

For Judith Ann Lee and the people of her tribe
—S.M.

ISBN 0-439-56148-5

Text copyright © 2003 by Kimberly Weinberger.
Illustrations copyright © 2003 by Stephen Marchesi.

12 11 10 9 8   7 8/0

Printed in the U.S.A.
First printing, November 2003

Let's Read About . . .
Pocahontas

by Kimberly Weinberger

Illustrated by Stephen Marchesi

Cartwheel
·B·O·O·K·S· ®

SCHOLASTIC INC.

New York   Toronto   London   Auckland   Sydney
Mexico City   New Delhi   Hong Kong   Buenos Aires

Pocahontas was born in Virginia in 1595.
She was a Native American princess.

Her father was a great chief named Powhatan.
He called his daughter Pocahontas because
the name means "playful."

Pocahontas did not go to school
as a young girl.
Children of her tribe were taught
by their parents.

Boys learned to hunt and fish.
Girls helped plant and gather food.

Pocahontas loved her home and the land
where she lived.
She did not know much about the world
beyond her village.

But all of that was about to change.

A captain named John Smith came
to Virginia in 1607.
He had sailed from England
with one hundred men.

Their pale skin and clothes were strange
to Pocahontas.

Chief Powhatan was not happy.
He was afraid that these strangers would take
his land.

One day, Powhatan's men came to take
John Smith to their town.
The chief wanted John Smith to know that
the tribe was strong.
He held a great feast.

The men and women would act out
a play during the feast.
The women would welcome John Smith
to the tribe.
They did this by pretending
to protect him from the men.
This was their way of making
the captain their friend.
Pocahontas was given a special role
to act out in the play.

The play began.
Chief Powhatan's men made believe
they were attacking Captain Smith.

Pocahontas pretended to protect John Smith.
She threw herself in front of the captain.
Now John Smith was a friend of the tribe.

So the English and the Native Americans
became friends.
The English did not know how to use
the land as the natives did.
Pocahontas brought corn, fish, and fur
to help them through the long, cold winter.

Captain Smith returned to England in 1609.
The friendship between the Native Americans
and the English began to fade.

Both sides started fighting over the land once again.

As the years passed, Pocahontas grew
into a beautiful young woman.

The English knew how much
Chief Powhatan loved his daughter.
So they took the princess away in 1613.

Pocahontas was held in a nearby town.
There she met an Englishman
named John Rolfe.
The two soon fell in love.

Pocahontas sent word to her father
that she wanted to marry John.
Chief Powhatan agreed.

The Native Americans and the English began
to trade goods once again.
Pocahontas had helped bring her people and
the English together for the second time.

Pocahontas and John soon had a son.
They named him Thomas.
The small family traveled to England
in 1616.

Pocahontas got to meet the King and Queen
of England.
She was surprised to see her old friend
John Smith there, too!

We remember Pocahontas today as a smart and brave woman who helped bring peace to her land.